Welcome!

Welcome to "Growing with Biblical Wisdom"! This guide is designed to help you incorporate biblical principles into your daily parenting. Each day features a summary title, a relevant scripture, and an explanation to teach your children. Our hope is that this guide will equip you with practical tools to raise your children with love, grace, and wisdom according to God's word.

Thank you for choosing "Growing with Biblical Wisdom" as a resource to help you raise your children in the ways of the Lord.

"Train up a child in the way he should go; even when he is old he will not depart from it." - Proverbs 22:6

Your support is crucial in continuing our work to spread God's message. We kindly ask you to consider leaving a 5-star review on Amazon to help us reach a wider audience. Your review not only increases our visibility but also serves as an inspiration to others seeking guidance and motivation.

We have included a convenient QR code below. Simply scan it, and you will be directed straight to the review page on Amazon. Your feedback is invaluable and plays a vital role in our mission to make a positive impact.

Contents

PARENTS GUIDE

- - - - - - - - - - -

Looking to the Bible to learn life lessons is valuable for several reasons. Firstly, the Bible is considered the inspired Word of God, containing wisdom and guidance that transcends time and culture. Its teachings offer timeless principles and values that can provide a solid foundation for navigating various aspects of life. By studying the Bible, we can gain insights into how to live with integrity, make wise decisions, cultivate healthy relationships, and find purpose and meaning in life.

Teaching our children that the answers to many life lessons are found in God's words can be approached in a way that resonates with their understanding and curiosity. Here are a few key points to consider:

Emphasize the Source of Wisdom: Explain that the Bible is not just a collection of stories but a book inspired by God, who knows and understands everything. Teach them that God's words hold timeless truths and practical guidance for living a fulfilling and righteous life.

Relate to Real-Life Examples: Use relatable examples from their everyday experiences to demonstrate how the principles and stories in the Bible apply to their own lives. Help them connect biblical teachings to situations they encounter, such as kindness, forgiveness, honesty, and empathy.

Encourage Exploration and Discussion: Encourage your children to explore the Bible by reading age-appropriate passages and stories together. Engage in open conversations about the lessons and values presented in the text. Ask them questions about their thoughts and interpretations, fostering their critical thinking skills and personal understanding.

Highlight the Impact of God's Word: Share stories and examples of individuals who have applied biblical principles in their lives and experienced positive transformations. Help your children understand that the Bible offers not only guidance but also hope, comfort, and inspiration.

Lead by Example: Demonstrate the importance of seeking wisdom from the Bible in your own life. Let your children see you reading and studying the Scriptures, applying its teachings, and sharing personal stories of how God's Word has influenced your decisions and actions.

By consistently incorporating these approaches, we can help our children recognize that the Bible is not just a book of rules, but a source of profound wisdom and guidance for every aspect of life. It is a book that reveals God's love, His desire for our well-being, and the path to a meaningful and purposeful life.

LESSON 1

love your neighbor

"Love your neighbor as yourself" - Matthew 22:39

Explanation:

Jesus teaches us to love others just as much as we love ourselves. This means we should treat others with kindness, respect, and care. We should always be thinking about how we can help others and make their lives better.

Conversation Starters:

How can we show love to our neighbors today?

Who is someone that you know that might need some help or encouragement?

How does it make you feel when someone shows you love and kindness?

JOURNAL

....

....

....

....

....

....

....

....

....

....

....

....

....

....

....

....

....

....

....

....

LESSON 2

the power of kindness

Be kind to one another, tenderhearted, forgiving one another, as God in Christ forgave you." - Ephesians 4:32

Explanation:

God wants us to be kind and compassionate to others, just as He is kind and compassionate to us. When we show kindness to others, we reflect God's love and character. We should always look for ways to be kind to those around us, even if it's just a small act of kindness.

Conversation Starters:

Can you think of a time when someone was kind to you? How did it make you feel?

How can we be kind to our family members and friends today?

Why do you think it's important to be kind to others?

JOURNAL

LESSON 3

the importance of honesty

"The Lord detests lying lips, but he delights in people who are trustworthy." - Proverbs 12:22

Explanation:

Honesty is an essential virtue in our lives. When we are truthful, we build trust with others and honor God's commandments. Honesty helps create strong bonds and fosters open communication within our families and communities.

Conversation Starters:

Why is it important to always tell the truth?

Have you ever been in a situation where it was difficult to be honest? How did you handle it?

How can we encourage honesty in our interactions with others?

JOURNAL

....

....

....

....

....

....

....

....

....

....

....

....

....

....

....

....

....

....

....

....

....

....

LESSON 4

gratitude for God's blessings

"Give thanks to the Lord, for he is good; his love endures forever." - 1 Chronicles 16:34

Explanation:

Expressing gratitude to God is an act of recognizing His blessings in our lives. Gratitude helps us cultivate a positive mindset, appreciate what we have, and develop a humble and content heart.

Conversation Starters:

What are some things you are grateful for in your life?

How can we show our gratitude to God for His love and blessings?

How does practicing gratitude make you feel?

JOURNAL

....

....

....

....

....

....

....

....

....

....

....

....

....

....

....

....

....

....

....

LESSON 5

the power of prayer

"Do not be anxious about anything, but in every situation, by prayer and petition, with thanksgiving, present your requests to God." - Philippians 4:6

Explanation:

Prayer is a way for us to communicate with God. It helps us find peace, seek guidance, and express our deepest desires and concerns. Through prayer, we invite God's presence into our lives and build a stronger relationship with Him.

Conversation Starters:

How does prayer make you feel?

What are some situations or challenges in your life where you think prayer can make a difference?

How can we make prayer a regular part of our daily lives?

JOURNAL

....
....
....
....
....
....
....
....
....
....
....
....
....
....
....
....
....
....
....

LESSON 6

trusting in God's plan

"Trust in the Lord with all your heart and lean not on your own understanding; in all your ways submit to him, and he will make your paths straight." - Proverbs 3:5-6

Explanation:

Trusting in God means having faith that He has a perfect plan for our lives, even when we don't understand what is happening. It involves surrendering our worries and uncertainties to Him and allowing Him to guide our steps.

Conversation Starters:

How can we trust in God's plan when things don't go the way we expect?

Can you think of a time when you had to trust God in a difficult situation? How did it turn out?

What are some ways we can remind ourselves to trust in God daily?

JOURNAL

....

....

....

....

....

....

....

....

....

....

....

....

....

....

....

....

....

....

....

LESSON 7

the importance of respect

"Show proper respect to everyone, love the family of believers, fear God, honor the emperor." - I Peter 2:17

Explanation:

Respect is a fundamental value that involves treating others with dignity, honor, and consideration. It encompasses respecting people's opinions, boundaries, and differences. By showing respect, we foster harmonious relationships and create a culture of understanding and acceptance.

Conversation Starters:

Why is it important to show respect to everyone, regardless of our differences?

Can you think of a time when you felt respected by someone? How did it impact your relationship with that person?

How can we demonstrate respect towards authority figures in our lives, such as teachers or elders?

JOURNAL

LESSON 8

the fruit of the spirit - joy

"But the fruit of the Spirit is love, joy, peace, forbearance, kindness, goodness, faithfulness." - Galatians 5:22

Explanation:

Joy is a fruit of the Holy Spirit and an essential aspect of our faith. It goes beyond temporary happiness and is rooted in our relationship with God. Joy can be experienced even in challenging circumstances and brings a sense of contentment and gratitude.

Conversation Starters:

What does joy mean to you? How is it different from happiness?

Can you think of moments when you felt a deep sense of joy? What brought about that joy?

How can we cultivate and share joy with others in our daily lives?

JOURNAL

LESSON 9

the golden rule

"So in everything, do to others what you would have them do to you, for this sums up the Law and the Prophets." - Matthew 7:12

Explanation:

The Golden Rule, as taught by Jesus, is a guiding principle for how we should treat others. It encourages empathy, kindness, and fairness. By treating others the way we want to be treated, we create a positive and respectful environment.

Conversation Starters:

What does the Golden Rule mean to you? Why is it important?

Can you share a situation where you applied the Golden Rule in your interactions with others?

How can we practice the Golden Rule in our everyday lives, both at home and in our community?

JOURNAL

....

....

....

....

....

....

....

....

....

....

....

....

....

....

....

....

....

....

....

....

....

LESSON 10

trusting God's timing

"But they who wait for the Lord shall renew their strength; they shall mount up with wings like eagles; they shall run and not be weary; they shall walk and not faint." - Isaiah 40:31

Explanation:

God's timing is perfect, even when it may not align with our own desires or expectations. Waiting on the Lord requires patience and trust in His plans, knowing that He will provide and guide us in due time.

Conversation Starters:

Why is it sometimes difficult to wait for things we want?

Can you think of a time when you had to wait for something, and it turned out better than expected?

How can we develop patience and trust in God's timing in our lives?

JOURNAL

....

....

....

....

....

....

....

....

....

....

....

....

....

....

....

....

....

....

LESSON 11

the gift of forgiveness

"Bear with each other and forgive one another if any of you has a grievance against someone. Forgive as the Lord forgave you." - Colossians 3:13

Explanation:

Forgiveness is a gift we give to others, just as God has forgiven us. It involves letting go of resentment, extending grace, and seeking reconciliation. Forgiveness frees us from the burden of anger and bitterness, fostering healing and restoring relationships.

Conversation Starters:

Why is forgiveness important in our relationships with others?

Can you think of a time when you had to forgive someone? How did it impact your relationship with that person?

How can we cultivate a forgiving heart and practice forgiveness in our daily lives?

26

JOURNAL

....

....

....

....

....

....

....

....

....

....

....

....

....

....

....

....

....

....

....

LESSON 12

the power of encouragement

"Therefore encourage one another and build one another up, just as you are doing." - I Thessalonians 5:11

Explanation:

Encouragement has the power to uplift, inspire, and motivate others. It involves offering kind words, support, and affirmation, helping people see their worth and potential. Through encouragement, we can make a positive impact on others' lives.

Conversation Starters:

How does it feel when someone encourages you?

Can you share a time when someone's encouragement made a difference in your life?

How can we be intentional in encouraging others and spreading positivity?

JOURNAL

....

....

....

....

....

....

....

....

....

....

....

....

....

....

....

....

....

....

LESSON 13

the power of contentment

"I have learned to be content whatever the circumstances."
- Philippians 4:11

Explanation:
Contentment is finding peace and satisfaction in what we have rather than constantly seeking more. It teaches us to appreciate the blessings in our lives and to trust that God's provision is enough.

Conversation Starters:
What are some things that make you feel content and grateful?

Why do you think it's important to be content with what we have?

How can we practice contentment in our daily lives?

JOURNAL

LESSON 14

the strength of perseverance

"Let us not become weary in doing good, for at the proper time we will reap a harvest if we do not give up." - Galatians 6:9

Explanation:

Perseverance is the ability to keep going, even in the face of challenges or obstacles. It teaches us resilience, determination, and the importance of not giving up on our goals and values.

Conversation Starters:

Can you think of a time when you had to persevere through a difficult situation?

Why is it important to keep trying, even when things get tough?

How can we support and encourage others to persevere?

JOURNAL

....

....

....

....

....

....

....

....

....

....

....

....

....

....

....

....

....

....

....

LESSON 15

the blessings of friendship

"A friend loves at all times, and a brother is born for a time of adversity." - Proverbs 17:17

Explanation:

Friendship is a precious gift from God. It provides companionship, support, and joy in our lives. True friends are there for us in both good times and challenging times, and they help us grow in love and character.

Conversation Starters:

What qualities do you value in a good friend?

Can you share a special memory or experience with a friend?

How can we be good friends to others and cultivate meaningful friendships?

JOURNAL

....

....

....

....

....

....

....

....

....

....

....

....

....

....

....

....

....

....

LESSON 16

the importance of self-control

"A person without self-control is like a city with broken-down walls." - Proverbs 25:28

Explanation:

Self-control is the ability to restrain our impulses, desires, and reactions. It helps us make wise decisions, resist temptations, and live a disciplined life. Self-control is a valuable virtue that leads to personal growth and healthy relationships.

Conversation Starters:

Can you think of a situation where practicing self-control would be beneficial?

Why is it important to think before we act or speak?

How can we develop self-control in our daily lives?

JOURNAL

....

....

....

....

....

....

....

....

....

....

....

....

....

....

....

....

....

....

LESSON 17

growing in faith through prayer

"Do not be anxious about anything, but in every situation, by prayer and petition, with thanksgiving, present your requests to God." - Philippians 4:6

Explanation:

Prayer is a powerful way to connect with God, seek His guidance, and find peace in the midst of challenges. It strengthens our faith, deepens our relationship with God, and allows us to experience His love and provision.

Conversation Starters:

How does prayer help you feel closer to God?

Can you share a time when prayer made a difference in your life?

How can we make prayer a regular part of our lives and seek God's will through it?

JOURNAL

....

....

....

....

....

....

....

....

....

....

....

....

....

....

....

....

....

....

LESSON 18

the impact of positive words

"Kind words are like honey—sweet to the soul and healthy for the body." - Proverbs 16:24

Explanation:

Our words have the power to uplift, encourage, and inspire others. Positive words can bring healing, joy, and hope to those around us. By choosing our words carefully, we can make a positive impact on people's lives.

Conversation Starters:

How does it feel when someone speaks kind and encouraging words to you?

Can you think of a time when someone's words made a difference in your day?

How can we use our words to spread positivity and build others up?

JOURNAL

LESSON 19

embracing God's grace

"For it is by grace you have been saved, through faith—and this is not from yourselves, it is the gift of God." - Ephesians 2:8

Explanation:
God's grace is His unmerited favor and love bestowed upon us. It is a free gift that we cannot earn or deserve. Embracing God's grace allows us to experience forgiveness, redemption, and a renewed relationship with Him.

Conversation Starters:
What does God's grace mean to you?

Can you think of a time when you experienced God's grace in your life?

How can we show gratitude for God's grace and extend grace to others?

JOURNAL

lined journal page

LESSON 20

the gift of generosity

"Each of you should give what you have decided in your heart to give, not reluctantly or under compulsion, for God loves a cheerful giver." - 2 Corinthians 9:7

Explanation:

Generosity involves freely sharing our time, talents, and resources with others. It reflects God's generous nature and blesses both the giver and the receiver. Through generosity, we can make a positive difference in the lives of others.

Conversation Starters:

What are some ways we can practice generosity in our daily lives?

How does it feel when we are generous towards others?

How can we cultivate a generous heart and prioritize giving to those in need?

JOURNAL

....
....
....
....
....
....
....
....
....
....
....
....
....
....
....
....
....
....
....

LESSON 21

the value of integrity

"The integrity of the upright guides them, but the unfaithful are destroyed by their duplicity." - Proverbs 11:3

Explanation:

Integrity is the quality of being honest, having strong moral principles, and doing what is right, even when no one is watching. It builds trust, earns respect, and reflects our commitment to living a life aligned with God's teachings.

Conversation Starters:

Why is integrity an important character trait to possess?

Can you share an example of someone you admire for their integrity?

How can we demonstrate integrity in our everyday choices and actions?

JOURNAL

LESSON 22

nurturing family relationships

"Honor your father and mother, so that you may live long in the land the Lord your God is giving you." - Exodus 20:12

Explanation:

Family relationships are a precious gift from God. They provide love, support, and a sense of belonging. Nurturing these relationships involves spending quality time together, communicating openly, and showing care and respect for one another.

Conversation Starters:

What are some ways we can strengthen our family relationships?

What are some of your favorite family traditions or activities?

How can we express love and appreciation to our family members?

JOURNAL

LESSON 23

nurturing family relationships

"For even the Son of Man did not come to be served, but to serve, and to give his life as a ransom for many." - Mark 10:45

Explanation:

Jesus taught us the importance of serving others selflessly. When we serve with a humble and compassionate heart, we reflect God's love and make a positive impact on those around us. Serving others brings joy, builds relationships, and glorifies God.

Conversation Starters:

Why do you think it's important to serve others?

Can you share a time when you felt fulfilled by serving someone?

How can we identify opportunities to serve in our community or within our circle of influence?

JOURNAL

....

....

....

....

....

....

....

....

....

....

....

....

....

....

....

....

....

....

....

LESSON 24

cultivating a heart of thankfulness

"Give thanks to the Lord, for he is good; his love endures forever." - Psalm 107:1

Explanation:
Cultivating a heart of thankfulness involves recognizing and appreciating the blessings in our lives. It shifts our focus from what we lack to what we have, fostering contentment, joy, and a deeper appreciation for God's goodness.

Conversation Starters:
What are some things you are grateful for today?

How does expressing gratitude impact your overall well-being?

How can we cultivate a habit of thankfulness in our daily lives?

JOURNAL

LESSON 25

honoring God with our talents

"Each of you should use whatever gift you have received to serve others, as faithful stewards of God's grace in its various forms." - 1 Peter 4:10

Explanation:

God has given each of us unique talents and abilities. When we use them to serve others and glorify God, we fulfill our purpose and contribute to the building of God's kingdom. Honoring God with our talents brings fulfillment and joy.

Conversation Starters:

What are some talents or abilities you feel God has blessed you with?

How can you use your talents to make a positive impact on others?

How can we encourage and support each other in discovering and using our God-given talents?

JOURNAL

LESSON 26

the beauty of creation

"The heavens declare the glory of God; the skies proclaim the work of his hands." - Psalm 19:1

Explanation:

The beauty and wonders of creation testify to God's power, creativity, and love. Observing and appreciating nature can deepen our awe of God and remind us of His presence in our lives. It invites us to be good stewards of the earth.

Conversation Starters:

What aspects of nature do you find most beautiful or awe-inspiring?

How does being in nature make you feel closer to God?

How can we take care of the environment and appreciate God's creation?

JOURNAL

LESSON 27

the power of perseverance

"Let us not become weary in doing good, for at the proper time we will reap a harvest if we do not give up." - Galatians 6:9

Explanation:

Perseverance is the ability to persist and endure in the face of challenges and setbacks. It is fueled by faith and the confidence that God is with us. Through perseverance, we can overcome obstacles and grow in character and faith.

Conversation Starters:

Can you share a time when you faced a challenge but persevered through it?

How does perseverance help us grow and develop resilience?

How can we rely on God's strength and guidance to persevere in difficult times?

JOURNAL

....

....

....

....

....

....

....

....

....

....

....

....

....

....

....

....

....

....

LESSON 28

the gift of contentment

"I know what it is to be in need, and I know what it is to have plenty. I have learned the secret of being content in any and every situation, whether well fed or hungry, whether living in plenty or in want." - Philippians 4:12

Explanation:
Contentment is finding satisfaction and peace in our current circumstances, trusting in God's provision and timing. It frees us from the grip of comparison and allows us to experience joy and gratitude in all situations.

Conversation Starters:
What does it mean to be content? How can we cultivate contentment in our lives?

Can you think of a time when you felt content and at peace despite challenging circumstances?

How can we shift our focus from what we lack to appreciating and being grateful for what we have?

JOURNAL

LESSON 29

walking in humility

"Do nothing out of selfish ambition or vain conceit. Rather, in humility value others above yourselves, not looking to your own interests but each of you to the interests of the others." - Philippians 2:3-4

Explanation:

Humility is the quality of having a modest and humble view of oneself. It involves putting the needs and interests of others before our own, valuing and serving them with a selfless heart.

Conversation Starters:

What does it mean to walk in humility? How can we cultivate humility in our lives?

Can you share an example of someone who embodies humility?

How can we demonstrate humility in our relationships with others, both at home and in the community?

JOURNAL

LESSON 30

trusting God's guidance

"Trust in the Lord with all your heart and lean not on your own understanding; in all your ways submit to him, and he will make your paths straight." - Proverbs 3:5-6

Explanation:

Trusting God's guidance means surrendering our own understanding and seeking His direction in every aspect of our lives. It requires faith and a willingness to follow His lead, knowing that He has our best interests at heart.

Conversation Starters:

Why is it important to trust in God's guidance? Can you share a personal experience of trusting God's direction?

How can we discern God's voice and seek His guidance in our decisions?

What are some ways we can demonstrate trust in God's plan, even when it's difficult or unclear?

JOURNAL

Parent's Guide

Values and Character Development

- Lesson 3: The Importance of Honesty
  - Facing the temptation to cheat on a test and choosing to be honest instead.
  - Admitting a mistake and taking responsibility for it, even if it means facing consequences.
  - Encouraging open and honest communication within the family, where everyone feels safe to share their thoughts and feelings.

- Lesson 9: The Golden Rule
  - Treating others with kindness and respect, just as you would like to be treated.
  - Resolving conflicts by putting yourself in the other person's shoes and seeking a mutually beneficial solution.
  - Encouraging empathy and understanding by discussing how certain actions or words might make others feel.

Parent's Guide

Gratitude and Appreciation

- Lesson 4: Gratitude for God's Blessings
  - Writing thank-you notes to express gratitude for gifts or acts of kindness.
  - Taking time each day to reflect on and appreciate the blessings in life, such as a loving family or good health.
  - Donating toys, clothes, or food to those less fortunate, recognizing the abundance in one's own life.
  -

- Lesson 21: Cultivating Thankfulness
  - Counting blessings and sharing them with the family during mealtime or bedtime routines.
  - Keeping a gratitude journal to write down things they are grateful for each day.
  - Expressing gratitude through words and actions, such as saying "thank you" and showing appreciation to others.

Parent's Guide

Emotional Intelligence and Self-Control

- Lesson 8: The Fruit of the Spirit - Joy
  - Choosing joy and gratitude in the face of challenges or disappointments.
  - Spreading joy by performing acts of kindness, such as surprising someone with a small gift or compliment.
  - Finding joy in the simple things, like spending quality time with family or enjoying nature's beauty.

- Lesson 26: Harnessing the Power of Self-Control
  - Managing anger or frustration in a healthy way, such as taking deep breaths or counting to ten.
  - Resisting the urge to engage in gossip or speak unkind words about others.
  - Practicing self-control in areas of temptation, such as limiting screen time or unhealthy snacking.

Parent's Guide
Faith and Trust

- Lesson 6: Trusting in God's Plan
  - Dealing with disappointment when not getting chosen for a team or a role in a school play.
  - Trusting that God has a purpose and plan during times of uncertainty, such as a family move or job change.
  - Letting go of worries and trusting that God will provide for the family's needs.

- Lesson 10: Trusting God's Timing
  - Waiting patiently for an answer to a prayer or a desired outcome.
  - Trusting that God has a plan for the future and understanding that His timing is perfect.
  - Finding peace in surrendering control and trusting in God's guidance.

Parent's Guide

Kindness and Empathy

- Lesson 2: The Power of Kindness
  - Witnessing or experiencing bullying and choosing to stand up for the person being bullied.
  - Performing random acts of kindness, such as leaving encouraging notes for others.
  - Offering assistance to someone in need, like helping carry groceries for an elderly neighbor.

- Lesson 23: Extending a Helping Hand
  - Visiting a nursing home or hospital to spend time with elderly or sick individuals.
  - Organizing a donation drive to collect essential items for those in need.
  - Volunteering at a local charity organization or participating in a community service project.

Parent's Guide

Forgiveness and Reconciliation

- Lesson 11: The Gift of Forgiveness
  - Forgiving a friend who has hurt your feelings or made a mistake.
  - Seeking forgiveness from someone you have wronged and taking steps to make amends.
  - Learning to let go of grudges and embracing the healing power of forgiveness.

- Lesson 25: Reconciling Differences
  - Resolving conflicts with siblings or friends through open communication and understanding.
  - Learning to listen and empathize with others' perspectives to find common ground.
  - Working towards reconciliation and rebuilding relationships that have been strained.

Parent's Guide

Encouragement and Support

- Lesson 12: The Power of Encouragement
  - Offering words of encouragement to a friend who is facing a difficult challenge.
  - Recognizing and appreciating the strengths and talents of others.
  - Providing support and motivation to someone pursuing their dreams or goals.

- Lesson 24: Building Others Up
  - Being a positive influence by offering kind words and uplifting compliments to classmates or siblings.
  - Supporting a family member or friend through a tough time by being there to listen and offer encouragement.
  - Celebrating the achievements and successes of others and genuinely expressing pride and happiness for them.

Parent's Guide

Decision-Making and Values

- Lesson 13: Making Wise Choices
  - Resisting peer pressure and making decisions aligned with personal values.
  - Seeking guidance from parents, mentors, or trusted adults when faced with difficult choices.
  - Considering the potential consequences before making a decision and thinking about how it aligns with one's faith.

- Lesson 30: Walking in Wisdom
  - Developing discernment and seeking wisdom in decision-making through prayer and seeking guidance from God.
  - Making choices that reflect godly values and principles, even when it may not be the popular or easy path.
  - Encouraging critical thinking and reflection on choices, weighing the long-term impact and aligning actions with faith.

Parent's Guide
Perseverance and Resilience

- Lesson 14: Embracing Resilience
  - Overcoming obstacles or setbacks and not giving up on goals or dreams.
  - Learning from failures or mistakes and using them as opportunities for growth.
  - Developing a positive mindset and embracing challenges as opportunities for personal development.

- Lesson 19: The Strength to Endure
  - Encouraging perseverance during challenging times, such as when facing a difficult school assignment or personal struggle.
  - Teaching the value of persistence in pursuing goals and dreams, even when faced with obstacles.
  - Sharing stories of individuals who have demonstrated resilience and discussing the lessons learned from their experiences.

Parent's Guide

Serving Others

- Lesson 15: Developing a Servant's Heart
  - Volunteering at a local shelter, food bank, or community service project.
  - Helping a neighbor with yard work or household chores without expecting anything in return.
  - Acts of kindness and service towards others, such as sharing toys or helping a classmate with their schoolwork.

- Lesson 27: Loving Our Neighbor
  - Exploring ways to show love and compassion to those in need, such as donating to a charity or supporting a cause.
  - Discussing the importance of being inclusive and reaching out to those who may feel lonely or left out.
  - Encouraging acts of kindness and service as a family, making it a regular part of daily life.

Parent's Guide

Self-Control and Emotional Management

- Lesson **26**: Harnessing the Power of Self-Control
  - Managing anger or frustration in a healthy way, such as taking deep breaths or counting to ten.
  - Resisting the urge to engage in gossip or speak unkind words about others.
  - Practicing self-control in areas of temptation, such as limiting screen time or unhealthy snacking.

- Lesson **16**: Taming the Tongue
  - Teaching the importance of using words wisely and avoiding hurtful or disrespectful language.
  - Exploring techniques to express emotions constructively, such as writing in a journal or talking with a trusted adult.
  - Cultivating empathy and understanding, helping children recognize the impact of their words on others.

Printed in Great Britain
by Amazon

41122407R00046